SOULFUL MUSINGS

Aishwarya Damodar

Qurate
quratebooks.com
Because everyone has a story to tell

Soulful Musings
Aishwarya Damodar

Published in 2024
© Published by

qurate
qratebooks.com

Qurate Books Pvt. Ltd.
Goa 403523, India
www.quratebooks.com
Tel: 1800-210-6527, Email: info@quratebooks.com

ISBN: 978-93-58985-41-2

Copyrights © 2024

The author is solely responsible for the content of this work, including all poems, themes, and expressions. Any resemblance to real persons, living or dead, or actual events is purely coincidental.

For permission requests, please contact the author at:
Aishwarya Damodar
Email: aaishwaryaa@gmail.com

Dedication

In loving memory of my dear father, Damodar. Your guidance and unwavering belief in me continue to shape my journey. I carry your memory in my heart as I share this work with the world, forever grateful for the lessons you taught me and the love you bestowed upon me.

And to my beloved mother, Bhakti, whose presence is a beacon of light in my life, illuminating even the darkest of days. Thank you for your endless support and faith in my dreams. This book is a testament to the love and resilience you've instilled in me.

Acknowledgement

With profound gratitude, I acknowledge those whose invaluable contributions have brought this poetry book to life:

To Joy Becker, whose friendship and perceptive insights sparked creativity and excitement throughout the writing process.

To Sudha Shenoy, my steadfast pillar, whose encouragement and enduring presence offered solace and resilience at every stage of my journey.

To Girish Nair, whose unwavering support and belief in me have made this book not just a reality, but a legacy.

Preface

The journey of writing my second book of poems, "Soulful Musings", was ignited by the overwhelmingly positive and encouraging reviews I received from readers of my debut collection, **"Inkspiration: A Collection of Poetic Musings"**. The heartfelt responses and profound connections my first book created inspired me to venture even deeper into the realms of poetic expression.

"Soulful Musings" is a profound journey we all undertake in our lives, though few of us pause to truly contemplate the essence of our existence, to reflect on its mysteries, and to marvel at the boundless possibilities that the future holds. This book begins with "Soulful Musings: Reflections", setting the stage for a deep and contemplative exploration of life, and concludes with "Soulful Musings: Beyond", inviting readers to look ahead with hope, curiosity, and an enlightened sense of wonder.

Through evocative verses and vivid imagery, this collection delves into themes of existential reflection, inner resilience, and the pursuit of meaning in an ever-changing world. With lyrical prose and heartfelt emotion, these poems capture the essence of the human spirit and celebrate the endless possibilities of the soul.

Embark with me on this poetic odyssey that aims to inspire, uplift, and leave a lasting imprint on your heart and mind. I hope that **"Soulful Musings"** will resonate with you as deeply as the experiences and emotions that inspired its creation.

Thank you for joining me on this journey. May these poems bring you moments of reflection, solace, and inspiration.

Aishwarya Damodar

Contents

The poem "Soulful Musings: Reflections" navigates the introspective journey of life, revealing truths and embracing the essence of existence in the quiet of the mind.

Soulful Musings: Reflections

In the quiet alcove where memories dwell,
where shadows dance and stories tell,
the journey unfolds in whispers soft,
of roads traversed and meanings sought.

Each moment a thread in life's grand design,
where trodden paths converge and twine,
revealing truth in patterns, aged and fine,
as life's reflections gracefully intertwine.

Through the lens of reflection, we see,
the mosaic of life's complexity,
in the stillness of the soul's gentle sway,
we embrace the beauty of each passing day.

As the stars above softly gleam,
we lose ourselves in the silent stream,
for in soulful musings, we come to find,
the essence of life in the quiet of mind.

INSPIRATIONAL

Poems that uplift and motivate, offering encouragement, hope, and strength.

The poem "Awakening" embraces the dawn of a new day, symbolizing the awakening of the soul and the promise of possibility that each sunrise brings.

Awakening

In the quiet hush before the dawn's embrace,
where shadows linger and dreams find their space,
a whisper stirs, a soft and gentle call,
a beckoning to awaken, to rise above all.

From slumber's depths, the soul begins to stir,
a yearning for light, for purpose to confer.
in the tender hues of the morning's first light,
a new chapter unfolds, dispelling the night.

With each breath drawn in the morning air,
comes a promise of possibility, beyond compare.
in the dew-kissed moments of the dawn's debut,
we find the courage to begin anew.

So, let us embrace this awakening within,
and let our hearts be open, new paths to begin.
for in every sunrise, there lies a tale untold,
a story of resilience, waiting to unfold.

The poem "Unlocking the Antidote" guides through life's chaos, unveiling tranquility in stillness, kindness, and shared joy—a beacon of enduring hope.

Unlocking the Antidote

In the chaos of life's stormy seas,
where shadows linger and doubts may tease,
we seek the light, the peace, the key,
to unlock the door to tranquility.

Amidst the clamor of daily strife,
we seek refuge from the trials of life,
in gentle whispers of inner peace,
where worries and fears find release.

It's found in laughter, in joy's bright hue,
in moments of stillness, where dreams renew,
in kindness shared and hearts made whole,
this antidote is for the searching soul.

In the dance of life's ebb and flow,
amongst the highs and depths below,
we find the antidote, serene and pure,
a beacon of hope that will endure.

The poem "Resilient Echoes" delves into the silent narratives of strength and resilience, capturing the unspoken sagas of courage and determination in every individual.

Resilient Echoes

In the quiet shadows where their stories reside,
untold sagas of strength in every stride.
Beneath composed exteriors, emotions entwined,
a reservoir of resilience in every mind.

They navigate challenges with wisdom in their eyes,
behind each resilient voice, a tale defies.
In the echoes, whispers of battles won,
chapters etched by the setting sun.

Through trials faced and tears they've shed,
a testament to the courage they embed.
With every step, a legacy weaves,
their voices, a symphony that resilience conceives.

For behind every individual's resounding voice,
a story echoes, a resolute choice.

The poem 'Time After Time' celebrates resilience and growth amidst life's changes.

Time After Time

In the face of change, we stand our ground,
amidst the chaos, a strength profound.
Through winds of fate and tides that churn,
in every twist, we find a lesson to learn.

In the face of change, we embrace the unknown,
with courage as our guide, seeds of resilience sown.
Through the ups and downs, the highs and lows,
in every challenge, our character grows.

In the face of change, we hold fast to hope,
with unwavering faith, we learn to cope.
Through darkest nights and storms that roar,
in every trial, we find the strength to soar.

For time after time, the light always shines on,
guiding our path, until the darkness is gone.
In the face of change, we rise, we're strong,
for time after time, we transform.

The poem "Could-Be's" explores the idea of embracing potential and pursuing reams rather than settling for missed opportunities.

Could-Be's

I'd rather be a -be, aiming for the sky,
than a might-have-been, stagnant, passing by.

For a could-be chases stars, dreams held high,
while a might-have-been fades, a silent sigh.

I'd rather be a has-been, with stories to share,
than a might-have-been, lost in stagnant air.

For a has-been once was, a memory rare,
while a might-have-been fades, without a care.

I'd rather be a could-be, reaching for the sky,
than a might-have-been, with dreams left to
die.

For in the pursuit of could-be, I'll always try,
leaving might-have-beens behind, to let them
fly.

TRANQUILITY

Poems that evoke peace, calmness, and serenity, inviting moments of quiet contemplation and reflection.

The poem "Vibrant Vistas" paints nature's beauty, where landscapes become vivid canvases, telling stories in vibrant hues, offering a timeless spectacle.

Vibrant Vistas

In meadows green and skies so wide,
nature's symphony, a radiant tide.
Each brushstroke tells a tale untold,
in colors vibrant, stories unfold.

Amidst the trees and rivers' flow,
nature's canvas, a timeless show.
No artist's hand, no poet's quill,
could capture nature's endless thrill.

From dawn's first light to evening's hue,
nature paints the world anew.
Each hue and shade, a masterpiece rare,
a breathtaking sight beyond compare.

In twilight's glow and forest's embrace,
nature's artistry finds its place.
A beauty divine, for all to see,
a glimpse of heaven's majesty.

The poem "Quietude's Quiescence" explores the serene tranquility of nature, where silence speaks volumes and solitude becomes a soothing melody, unveiling the essence of life in its stillness.

Quietude's Quiescence

... and, into the hills I tread,
to free my mind, where silence bled,
seeking the core, where truths unfold,
in nature's arms, my soul enrolled.

The quietness was deafening,
a canvas of echoes, whispers, and more,
where thoughts spoke in hushed refrain,
and solitude danced in the quiet's core.

The quietness was chaotic,
a storm of calm, a paradoxical play,
where tranquility wore a turbulent guise,
and serenity thrived in the disarray.

The quietness was calming,
a lullaby sung by the mountain air,
where peace embraced each weary sigh,
and solace found me, unaware.

... and, thus, into the hills when I went,
I found my soul, in quiet's descent,
a journey profound, a silence profound,
where the essence of life in stillness was found.

The poem "Zephyr's Touch" celebrates the soothing embrace of the gentle breeze, offering solace and serenity amidst life's chaos.

Zephyr's Touch

Zephyr, a balm for weary souls,
in its gentle touch, serenity unfolds.
A respite from the day's relentless toll,
in its embrace, we find console.

Amidst the chaos, Zephyr's grace,
whispers of peace in its gentle trace.
A moment's pause, a fleeting space,
with each soft sigh, worries find solace.

In its tender breeze, troubles efface,
Zephyr's embrace, a tranquil grace.
In its gentle dance, hearts find their way,
a blissful respite from life's disarray.

The poem "Tranquil Waters" invites you to experience the serene and ever-flowing beauty of calm waters.

Tranquil Waters

A soothing peace that seems to grow,
Tranquil Waters, have you felt their flow?
Where sunlight dances on the tide,
secrets whispered, always to confide.

Beneath the sky's expansive dome,
Tranquil Waters find a home.
Ever-changing, yet steadfastly serene,
in their depths, a world unseen.

Where memories linger in the air,
Tranquil Waters, calm and fair.
Flowing onward, a timeless sight,
echoes in symphony, day and night.

Reflecting serenity in every hue,
Tranquil Waters, forever renew.

The poem "Seize Moments" urges you to embrace life's fleeting beauty, treasure each precious moment, and fill your memories with joy and fulfillment.

Seize Moments

In life's brief passage, swiftly ablaze,
live each moment, in joy's bright rays.
For life's a tale, swiftly unfurled,
with each breath a gem, in this precious world.

Laugh with the sun, dance with the moon,
embrace the stars, in the night's soft croon.
With every step, paint colors anew,
in the canvas of life, make dreams come true.

Life's a fleeting gift, a treasure to hold,
cherish its moments, more precious than gold.
For in the end, when all is said and done,
may memories of joy be the legacy you've spun.

The poem "Everyday Magic" revels in life's simple joys inviting readers to savor the enchantment of everyday moments.

Everyday Magic

In a cup of tea, a universe blooms,
whispering tales in quiet rooms.
Raindrops tap on the window's glass,
sharing secrets as moments pass.

A cat's stretch, a morning's song,
in dawn's embrace, where dreams belong.
Books stacked high, their stories known,
each page a journey, all on its own.

A single flower in a weathered vase,
embracing beauty, in any case.
Moonlight spills across the floor,
inviting dreams to explore once more.

In simple moments, life's treasures reside,
in quirks and rhythms, where stories hide.
Pause and listen, in this everyday space,
discover the magic, in each quirky trace.

EXISTENTIAL

Poems delving into the depths of being, pondering the mysteries of life, meaning, and purpose, exploring existential questions.

The poem "Unplugged Bliss" celebrates the tranquility found in disconnecting from the digital world and embracing the richness of offline moments.

Unplugged Bliss

In the quiet of dawn's soft glow,
where screens lie dark and silent, low,
A world untouched by digital fray,
Offline, where moments gently sway.

No buzzing alerts, no endless scroll,
just the whisper of wind, the song of soul,
In unplugged hours, time finds its pace,
a sanctuary from the digital race.

Offline, where the real world gleams,
in the touch of a hand, in shared dreams,
Where conversations flow, face to face,
each moment cherished, each memory traced.

In this oasis of stillness, we find,
the true luxury of an offline mind,
Where presence reigns and connections thrive,
in the richness of life, truly alive.

So let us unplug, let us unwind,
and savor the luxury of offline time,
For in the quiet moments, we rediscover,
the joy of being, fully, deeply, together.

The poem "Shadows and Light: Doubt and Faith" delves into the intricate interplay between doubt and faith within the human psyche.

Shadows and Light: Doubt and Faith

In the heart's chamber, doubt and faith collide,
a boundless battle where truths abide.
Doubt whispers softly, weaving threads of fear,
while faith stands steadfast, its presence clear.

In the labyrinth of uncertainty's maze,
doubt casts shadows, obscuring hopeful rays.
Yet faith, a beacon, guides through darkest night,
igniting hope with its unwavering light.

Through trials and tribulations, doubts may sway,
but faith's resilience keeps fears at bay.
For in the forge of life's relentless test,
faith emerges triumphant, ever blessed.

In the crucible of choice, where paths diverge,
doubt may beckon, its voice a haunting dirge.
Yet faith, a fortress, stands firm and tall,
guiding the soul, through doubts' relentless squall.

The poem "Embers of Flame: A Phoenix's Rise" captures the empowering essence of rising above challenges, embracing healing, and the newfound freedom to forge a brighter future.

Embers of Flame: A Phoenix's Rise

In the smoldering embers of a hurtful past,
her heart, ablaze, consumes the pain at last.
Burning memories to ashes, a fierce release,
she emerges from the flames, seeking inner
peace.

Through the scorching trials that once held her
tight,
she strides forward, embracing the healing light.
The scars may linger, but she wears them with
grace,
a testament to strength in the newfound space.

A phoenix rising from the fiery demise,
she moves on, a resolute spirit, wise.
No longer captive to the shadows that cast,
she steps into a future, free at last.

The poem "Embracing Life" explores the journey of finding purpose and resilience amidst life's challenges.

Embracing Life

In the shadows of expectation, I once stood,
longing for a life that felt truly good.
Believing in a future, yet to be unfurled,
where dreams would dance, and joys would
whirl.

But the days slipped by, tasks stacked high,
a constant race against the ticking of the sky.
Always something to achieve, to grasp, to
attain,
leaving my true essence adrift in the mundane.

I yearned for a beginning, a fresh start,
where passion ignited and purpose stole my
heart.
Yet amidst the chaos, a truth emerged clear,
these hurdles, these challenges, were my life's
frontier.

Each obstacle surmounted, each battle fought,
shaped the contours of the life I sought.
They were not barriers, but guides along the
way,
leading me closer to the dawn of a brighter day.

So, I embrace the journey, the twists and turns,
for they are the fabric from which my life learns.
In each trial and triumph, I find my true stride,
for this journey is where my real life resides.

The poem "The Divided Muse" explores the complex essence of a being torn between celestial grace and infernal whispers.

The Divided Muse

In twilight's embrace, she roamed,
half-goddess, half-hell, her essence sown.
Celestial grace, infernal whispers cling,
her duality a celestial ring.

Warmth of fire, chill of abyss,
in her touch, realms intertwist.
Laughter echoes, stories untold,
within her, mysteries unfold.

Through light and shadow, she strides,
a paradox in cosmic tides.
Soul divided, yet whole in her grace,
dancing between realms, in infinite space.

The poem "The Unstoppable She: Chaos in Motion" celebrates a spirited woman, navigating life with unpredictability and leaving a trail of joy in her wake.

The Unstoppable She: Chaos in Motion

She's a whirlwind, a force of nature,
leaving chaos in her wake, without fail.
With a mind like a rollercoaster,
and a heart that sets sail.

In a world of predictability,
She's the unexpected twist.
With a laugh that's infectious,
and a spirit that can't resist.

She trips over her own two feet,
but always manages to land on her toes.
With a knack for turning mishaps into feats,
She's the queen of unforeseen throws.

In the game of life, she's a wildcard,
a walking contradiction, full of surprise.
But when the dust settles and the cards are starred,
She's the one who's got that sparkle in her eyes.

So here's to the unstoppable She,
with her laughter echoing down the hall.
For in a world of chaos and glee,
She's the one who makes it all.

The poem "Journeying Mindscapes" explores the evolution of the human mind across different stages of life.

Journeying Mindscapes

In minds so young, where innocence reigns,
imagination blooms, free from chains.
Whispers of wonder, secrets untold,
in the playground of youth, dreams take hold.

Through adolescent minds, where passions ignite,
navigating emotions, in the quest for light.
Echoes of rebellion, yet to take flight,
in the teenage heart, the world feels bright.

In adult minds, where responsibilities weigh,
seeking purpose and meaning, day by day.
Unraveling truths, in the search for grace,
in the complexities of life, finding one's place.

In minds seasoned by time, at life's twilight,
echoes of wisdom, in the fading light.
Whispers of reflection, secrets unfold,
in the sunset of life, stories are told.

The poem "Zendagi Migzara" reflects on the passage of time and the resilience of the human spirit in the face of loss and change.

Zendagi Migzara

In the corridors of memory, echoes fade,
past smiles linger, yet elude the cascade.
Grief surrenders, yielding to dawn's embrace,
fear disperses, leaving only grace.

Tears, silent witnesses of time's traverse,
etched in the eye's reflection, they converse.
In Dad's departure, joy succumbed to mourn,
yet Zendagi Migzara whispered, Life Goes On.

In life's canvas, woven with threads untold,
emotions dance, in hues vibrant and bold.
Amidst the labyrinth, stand steadfast and
strong,
for Zendagi Migzara, the soul's resilient song.

The poem "Tranquilizing Silence" invites readers to embrace the tranquility within to find solace and renewal amidst life's tumultuous currents.

Tranquilizing Silence

In the depths of the soul, where healing takes flight,
whispered truths dance in the soft moonlight.
Yet amidst the chaos of the mind's array,
finding stillness becomes the soul's sway.

Within tranquil echoes, wisdom finds its voice,
a sanctuary where spirits rejoice.
To listen, one must quiet the mind's roar,
unlocking the door to serenity's core.

In the gentle embrace of silence profound,
where healing melodies of peace are found,
Embrace the quiet, let its essence unfurl,
revealing the soul's capacity to heal and swirl.

The poem "Solitary Serenade" delves into the profound experience of solitude, portraying it as a journey of self-discovery and inner peace amidst the vast expanse of life's uncertainties.

Solitary Serenade

In the depths of solitude, I roam,
a captain of my solitary sea.
Beneath the vast expanse of sky and foam,
I navigate the currents, wild and free.

No lover's call, no distant plea,
just the whispered song of destiny.
In the quiet expanse, where shadows flee,
I find solace in my solitary sea.

In the tempest of calm, chaos unfolds,
a paradoxical dance, both fierce and serene.
Within the depths, where silence holds,
I find tranquility in the quiet unseen.

So, I embrace the solitude, serene and true,
in the silence, I find myself anew.
For in the depths of my solitary sea,
I discover the strength to simply be.

INTROSPECTION

Poems exploring personal truths and insights through deep self-reflection.

The poem "A Stranger's Rhapsody" explores the sensation of feeling like an outsider in one's own life, yet ultimately finding inner harmony and acceptance amidst the journey of self-discovery.

A Stranger's Rhapsody

In the depths of the night, a solitary soul,
lost in the echoes of a distant toll,
wandering through shadows, grappling with
strife.
Ever felt like a stranger in your own life?

Yet, amidst the chaos, a flicker of light,
a phoenix rising from the ashes of inner strife.
with every heartbeat, a familiar fife,
Ever felt like a stranger in your own life?

A symphony of self, a melody adorned,
no longer a stranger, but in harmony rife.
embracing the journey, finding peace and life.
Ever felt like a stranger in your own life?

The poem "Whispers Beyond Words" delves into the ineffable nature of human emotions, exploring the limitations of language in expressing the depth and complexity of inner feelings.

Whispers Beyond Words

In quiet corners where emotions reside,
no matter how many quotes you read, abide,
some feelings linger, untamed and still,
defying language, where words go wrong.

Among lyrics that dance in the air,
songs echo sentiments, beyond compare,
yet, in the melange of phrases, a subtle despair,
emotions elusive, floating like the air.

As ink dances on the parchment white,
a reminder that emotions take flight,
beyond the verses and the lines that twirl,
sometimes, words can't capture the unfurl.

In echoes of silence, where emotions conceal,
no matter how many quotes you read, surreal,
sometimes, the heart's language, too profound,
eludes the essence that words expound.

The poem "Sight's Epiphany" unfolds a journey through life's twists and turns, where moments of blindness lead to profound insights and inner

Sight's Epiphany

In the rhythm of time, where shadows dance,
I wandered through moments, took a chance.
In the canvas of life, threads so bright,
I lost my sight, I gained insight.

Through the twists and turns, the highs and
lows,
life's melody played, its beats it chose.
Blind to the future, yet wisdom in flight,
I lost my sight, I gained insight.

In the silence of solitude, whispers profound,
echoes of understanding, a soul unbound.
The dark may cloak, yet the heart feels the
light,
I lost my sight, I gained insight.

So let the stars twinkle in the vast night sky,
a constellation of lessons learned, reaching nigh.
For in the absence of vision, a new vision takes
flight,
I lost my sight, I gained insight.

The poem "Uncharted Horizons" invites readers on a journey of exploration and adventure, beckoning them to embrace the unknown with courage and determination as they venture into new territories.

Uncharted Horizons

Eyes seek,
the first light's gleam,
where horizons stretch,
beyond our dream.

Infinite expanse,
calling out,
to those who dare,
to those who doubt.

Whispers soft,
from winds untamed,
beckon forth,
the brave, unnamed.

Step by step,
into the void,
undaunted hearts,
are deployed.

For in the uncharted,
lies the thrill,
of discovery,
beyond our will.

The poem "Unraveling Shadows" explores the journey of self-discovery amidst anxiety and uncertainty, finding solace and revelation in moments of stillness and solitude.

Unraveling Shadows

In the labyrinth of thoughts, anxiety takes its twirl,
a dance of uncertainties, where the mind begins to unfurl.
Yet to encounter the essence, the real within,
embarking on a journey, a quest about to begin.

In the rush of a swift, ephemeral ride,
moments slip like sand on life's ceaseless tide.
Yet the twilight endures an inviting exploration,
where shadows unveil secrets, an ethereal revelation.

The luminescence's gentle embrace, a comforting shroud,
as the soul unfolds, silent and proud.
Beneath the celestial bodies, in profound stillness,
discovering self, in the quietest sound's brilliance.

In the hushed sanctuary where tranquility reigns,
the true self emerges from the shadows' chains.
Amidst chaos or in solitude's tender grace,
I'll meet the real me in every embrace.

The poem "I AM..." delves into the complexities of self-discovery, portraying the journey through silence, chaos, and introspection.

I AM...

In the silence of dawn, I am the whisper,
echoing through the chambers of my soul.
I am the seeker, the wanderer, the dreamer,
embarking on a journey towards the whole.

In the stillness of night, I am the shadow,
dancing with the echoes of forgotten dreams.
I am the question, the answer, the essence,
unraveling the mysteries of unseen streams.

In the chaos of day, I am the silence,
a tranquil oasis in the midst of noise.
I am the strength, the resilience, the beacon,
guiding towards inner peace and poise.

I am the sum of all that I believe,
a mosaic woven with threads of light and dark.
I am the canvas, the artist, the creation,
painting my existence with colors stark.

REFLECTION

Poems exploring contemporary issues and personal experiences, prompting contemplation on relationships, society, and challenges.

The poem "Digital Divide" delves into the paradox of modern connectivity, exploring how the digital realm both connects and isolates us from genuine human interaction.

Digital Divide

In the glow of screens, our worlds collide,
as pixels replace the warmth by our side.
In the digital embrace, we find our retreat,
but lose the touch of those we used to meet.

Through cyberspace we roam, endlessly
scrolling,
in search of connection, our hearts are
consoling.
Yet as we type away, lost in the virtual throng,
we forget the voices that once kept us strong.

Friends reduced to avatars, faces unknown,
as we pour our hearts out to the void alone.
We share our lives in pixels and bytes,
but miss the laughter on shared moonlit nights.

In the web's tangled threads, we lose our way,
forgetting the joy of a sunlit day.
Our screens hold us close, but keep us apart,
from the beating hearts that once filled our
heart.

So let us unplug, and reclaim the time,
to bridge the gap in this digital climb.
For amidst the pixels and virtual air,
it's the touch of loved ones that truly care.

The poem "Eventide Solitude" portrays the yearning of parents for the presence of their grown child, reflecting on the emptiness of their home and the enduring love that remains.

Eventide Solitude

In the silent echoes of our empty nest,
where once your laughter brought us zest,
We search for traces of your presence,
but find only shadows, devoid of essence.

In our arms, you were a warmth so bright,
a beacon of hope, a comforting light.
Through life's storms, we stood by your side,
nurturing your dreams, with steadfast pride.

Now as we age, our steps grow slow,
in solitude, the shadows grow.
We don't ask for riches or gold,
just the warmth of your hand as we grow old.

So, hear this plea from hearts laid bare,
don't leave us to solitude's despair.
For in the embrace of family, we find our worth,
a treasure beyond measure, the truest hearth.

The poem "Reflection's Resonance" delves into the profound impact of introspection, unveiling the transformative power of self-reflection in shaping one's perception of the world.

Reflection's Resonance

Agitation whispers in the corridors of the mind,
I'm yet to seek myself, a journey undefined.
The day has waltzed by in swift delight,
but there is still the night in moonlight.

In the melody's embrace, a distant hum,
lost in the vast world, still becoming one.
I hear the unspoken words I shelve,
secrets mirrored, in the reflections I delve.

The sky extends its cosmic hand,
wishes unfurl, thoughts scattered like sand.
If I pause, listen to my silent plea,
I'll carry myself into my life's mystery.

Agitation echoes, a relentless rhyme,
I'm yet to find the core of this soulful climb.
The day retires, leaves its fleeting light,
yet, there is still the night, a realm infinite.

The poem "Melancholy's Touch" delves into the embrace of melancholia, exploring its profound melodies and shadows.

Melancholy's Touch

In melancholia's embrace, a melody,
a symphony of thoughts begins to play,
unraveling mysteries with gentle grace,
as shadows dance in the light of day.

In melancholia's sway, the mind awakes,
in moments of silence, wisdom takes flight,
its hold, a journey through shadowed lakes,
a pathway to understanding, pure and bright.

In melancholia's grasp, springs creativity,
a canvas for the soul's vivid hues to paint,
within its hold, we find serenity,
a sanctuary where dreams and visions acquaint.

So, do not fear melancholy's touch,
for within its realm, lies beauty's clutch.

The poem "In Her Own Way" narrates the journey of a resilient soul who, despite facing unexpected challenges, finds the courage to carve her path and shape her destiny according to her own will.

In Her Own Way

She went her own way, with dreams in her eyes,
ambitions high, beneath boundless skies.
Yet fate had plans, a different course to devise,
leading her astray, under unforeseen ties.

She halted, amidst life's turbulent stream,
in the chaos, seeking a quiet gleam.
Reflecting on paths, lost in the extreme,
where her mind worked, in silent scheme.

INTERLUDE

With whispered courage, she rose from the still,
determined to rewrite her life's will.
In her own way, she shaped her destiny's flight,
her will and fate entwined, with newfound
might.

The poem "Randomness" reflects on the frantic pace of modern life, where amidst the hustle and bustle, individuals often lose sight of their true selves.

Randomness

In the rush of today's hurried strife,
lost in the shuffle of city life.
Masks conceal, but truth evades,
in the randomness, our essence fades.

Each step we take, a frantic race,
but do we truly know our place?
Lost in screens, we stumble blind,
in the whirlwind, our peace we find.

In this era of speed and haste,
we're trapped in a relentless chase.
Yearning for simplicity's embrace,
but caught in life's relentless race.

The poem "Eclipsed" delves into the shifting dynamics between generations, as traditional values give way to new norms, leaving behind a sense of uncertainty and loss.

Eclipsed

In the dance of time, a shift unseen,
values once held, now in-between.
Between two worlds, a divide revealed,
as echoes of tradition are slowly concealed.

Eclipsed, the notion of staying close,
as roles reverse, and new paths propose.
From "I stay with my parents" to "They stay with
me",
a transformation witnessed, for all to see.

Generations apart, yet connected by thread,
what once was revered, now questioned instead.
As independence blooms and norms adapt,
the old ways fade, like a worn-out map.

But in the eclipse of tradition, a void is found,
as old convictions wane, no longer profound.
Amidst shifting norms, a silence surrounds,
where once cherished values now confound.

FREEDOM

Poems reflecting on personal liberation, breaking free from constraints and embracing individuality.

The poem "Into the Unknown: A Captain's Sojourn" embarks on a journey of self-discovery and courage, as the protagonist sets sail into uncharted waters.

Into the Unknown: A Captain's Sojourn

In the quiet realm where doubts subside,
a realization, like a rising tide.
No more to lose, no unwelcoming shore,
You stand at a threshold, uncertainty no more.

A ship untethered, in the vast expanse,
freedom whispers, takes its chance.
No hesitation, no lingering fear,
the captain within, strong and clear.

Through uncharted waters, you will set sail,
the narrative will be rewritten, as a vibrant tale.
No anchor of doubt, no chains to bind,
the captain's spirit, resolute in mind.

With no shadows gnawing, no past confined,
your free-spirit you will surely find.
For in the open sea, where dreams are unfurled,
YOU are the captain, the master of your world.

The poem "Finding Ground" depicts a journey of resilience, where the protagonist discovers both wings to soar and roots to ground amidst life's trials.

Finding Ground

In the labyrinth of trials,
worn and thin;
She sought her wings,
a surge within.

Through trials' maze,
where hope was found;
She rose with wings,
her spirit unbound.

Amidst the skies,
a celestial sound;
yet, within the clouds,
her roots were found.

In soaring high, and
standing sound
She found her wings, and
grounded ground.

The poem "Belonging Boundlessly" celebrates the journey of a free-spirited soul finding solace and truth in the untamed embrace of nature.

Belonging Boundlessly

In her wanderlust's embrace,
she found her sanctuary, her solace,
as boundless as the flowing river's grace,
with no beginning, no end, just space.

Her wild spirit knew no confines,
fearless, she danced under cosmic signs,
bathing in her own radiant shine,
melding with the Universe divine.

She belonged to the untamed breeze,
to the whispered secrets of ancient trees,
her essence woven in the dance of seas,
a nomad soul, embracing freedoms keys.

In her belonging, she found her truth,
unbound by chains of age or youth,
for in her wildness, she found her proof
that belonging to oneself is the ultimate sooth.

The poem "Carte Blanche" celebrates the liberating journey of embracing life as a blank canvas, where limitless possibilities await, and fears dissolve in the realm of pure potentiality.

Carte Blanche

In the canvas of life, a blank slate appears,
Carte Blanche whispers, shedding all fears.
No boundaries constrain, no limits in sight,
a realm of possibilities, bathed in pure light.

With freedom unleashed, like wings taking
flight,
Carte Blanche beckons, igniting delight.
Each stroke of destiny, a brushstroke divine,
crafting a masterpiece, on the canvas of time.

With courage, we dance into the unknown,
Carte Blanche's embrace, where hopes are sown.
To paint our aspirations boldly, with colors so
bright,
Carte Blanche empowers, to shape our own
light.

The poem "Stop Waiting" urges you to take charge of your destiny, to break free from the confines of waiting for external validation or perfect timing, and instead just seize the moment.

Stop Waiting

Stop waiting for the clock to dictate,
your destiny is yours, it's never too late.

Stop waiting for the winds to shift,
take charge, let your spirits lift.

Stop waiting for permissions to chase,
life's treasures, don't let them erase.

Stop waiting for the world's applause,
your dreams are worthy, break through the pause.

Stop waiting for tomorrow's rhyme,
embrace today, it's your time to shine.

Stop waiting to explore on your own,
in uncharted realms, your seeds are sown.

Don't hesitate or stall, just heed the call,
seize the moment, seize it all.

The poem "Winds of Change" embodies the resilience and adaptability of the human spirit in the face of change.

Winds of Change

In winds of change, our spirits rise,
as pivots shift, and courage defies.

Through turbulent skies, we chart our way,
embracing the challenge, come what may.

With every gust, we find a chance to grow,
to spread our wings, and gracefully soar.

No path too daunting, no challenge too grand,
amidst the shifting winds, we take our stand.

For in the Winds of Change, our Wings are
found,
as we journey onward, unafraid, unbound.

EXPLORATION

Poems that embrace the spirit of discovery, venturing into uncharted territories with curiosity and courage.

The poem "Attraversiamo, Mom" is a daughter's loving invitation to her aging mother to explore new horizons together, leaving behind the past and embracing the journey ahead, hand in hand.

Attraversiamo, Mom

In the whispers of twilight's glow,
Attraversiamo, let's together go.
Hand in hand, hearts intertwined,
leave the past, our souls aligned.

Across the bridge of dreams we'll tread,
with every step, old burdens shed.
Forsaking pain, embracing light,
together, we'll conquer the darkest night.

Through fields of hope, where flowers bloom,
Attraversiamo, let's leave the gloom.
Into the unknown, we boldly stride,
in each other's love, we'll find our guide.

So let's cross over, you and I,
beyond the tears, beneath the sky.
For in our journey, we'll discover anew,
the boundless joy of me and you.

The poem "The Path's Plea" beckons travelers to heed the call of the winding road, urging them to venture forth despite uncertainty.

The Path's Plea

Upon the winding road, the path does plead,
"Traveler, heed my call, follow where I lead."
For in the journey's stride, secrets lie untold,
only by venturing forth shall they unfold.

Stop not, for even when the way seems obscure,
the path whispers softly, steadfast and sure.
One last time, press on with unwavering might,
for in perseverance, you'll find the guiding light.

Through valleys hushed and mountains tall,
the path awaits, urging one and all.
Each step taken, a story to unveil,
in the journey's rhythm, the heart sets sail.

So heed the call of the path that implores,
embrace the journey, open new doors.
For in the quest for what lies ahead,
lies the essence of life, where dreams are fed.

The poem "Exploring the Unexplored" invites us to embrace the unknown, urging us to step into uncharted territories where mysteries await discovery.

Exploring the Unexplored

Step by step,
into the unknown,
where mysteries lie,
waiting to be honed.

Infinite realms,
beyond the known,
beckoning souls,
to journeys alone.

Whispers call,
from distant shores,
urging us forth,
to explore, to soar.

Unyielding hearts,
forge paths untrod,
embracing the challenge,
of the unexplored nod.

For in the exploration,
beyond the known,
lies the essence of life,
forever to be owned.

The poem "Predictably Unpredictable" celebrates the colorful complexity of an individual who joyfully embraces life's uncertainties, defying expectations with her enigmatic nature.

Predictably Unpredictable

In her whirlwind being, a colorful spectacle,
she weaves hues diverse, each respectable.
A canvas of quirks, universes to enable,
she's predictably unpredictable, beautifully
parable.

Her laughter echoes, joyful and profound,
chaos embraced, her essence unbound.
Unfazed by futures uncertain, unable to label,
she remains predictably unpredictable.

With each glance, a new surprise,
in her gaze, the universe lies.
A mosaic of contradictions, undeniable,
in her essence, predictably unpredictable.

In her enigmatic dance, life's eternal riddle,
predictably unpredictable, in the middle.

The poem "Rhyme of Serendipity" explores the enigmatic dance between fate and chance, revealing the unseen threads of destiny and the whispers of hope that weave through life's labyrinth.

Rhyme of Serendipity

In time's labyrinth,
a serenade, a rhyme,
Pages unfold unseen,
destiny, a whispering mime.

Is it or is it not,
life's ethereal stream,
Where did I end up,
lost in a dream?

Was it or was it not,
a dream's soft gleam,
In serendipity's dance,
fate's gentle seam.

Whispers of hope,
in the night's moonbeam,
Mystery weaves,
a tale to dream.

The poem "Twistedness" whimsically explores the delightful eccentricities of life while seeing the world through a uniquely twisted lens.

Twistedness

In a world of curious turns and bends,
twistedness into our lives descends.
Like pretzels, we dance with delight,
in every twist, a new insight.

With humor as odd as the moon's bright gleam,
twistedness becomes our cherished theme.
Through eyes askew, the world we view,
finding beauty in the askew.

In tangled thoughts, where laughter's free,
twistedness becomes our glee.
For in life's twists, we truly find,
the joy that lies in the unconfined.

The poem "Dream On..." inspires the reader to never cease dreaming, emphasizing the role of dreams in expanding one's horizons and unlocking potential.

Dream On...

Dream on, dear heart, with eyes aglow,
in the quiet of night's tender flow,
let dreams weave tales of wonder and delight,
guiding you through the darkest night.

Dream on, with hope's soft refrain,
in dreams, find solace from life's mundane,
for dreams are the whispers of your soul,
leading you where your heart finds its role.

Dream on, dear soul, with spirit bold,
in dreams, find courage to break the mold,
for dreams are the keys to unlock your might,
igniting the fire within to take flight.

Dream on, with passion's fervent call,
in dreams, find strength to stand tall,
for dreams are the echoes of your truest desire,
leading you higher to aspirations you aspire.

The poem "Gratitude" cherishes life's blessings, from each breath to the warmth of human connection, urging us to appreciate the beauty in every moment.

Gratitude

In the tapestry of life, woven with care,
are moments of joy, beyond compare.
For the gift of breathing, we're truly blessed,
each inhale a reminder of life's endless zest.

The sight of a sunrise, painting the sky,
a symphony of colors that lifts us high.
The scent of a flower, carried on the breeze,
filling our souls with tranquil ease.

The sound of laughter, ringing clear,
a melody of happiness, drawing near.
The touch of a loved one, gentle and kind,
a connection that warms both heart and mind.

To love and be loved, an eternal flame,
kindling hope and easing life's pain.
To care for another, in times of need,
a selfless act, born of goodwill and deed.

And in the act of giving, we receive,
a bond of humanity that helps us believe.
For life's greatest joy, in all its giving,
is found in the gratitude of truly living.

As nature's masterpiece, we stand in awe,
grateful for the wonders life foresaw.
For in every moment, big or small,
we find reasons to give thanks, one and all.

The poem "Soulful Musings: Beyond" invites the reader to believe in the mystery and magic of the undiscovered realms ahead, urging them to be in awe of the times to come as newer meanings await in the unfolding paradigms.

Soulful Musings: Beyond

Beyond the known, beyond the seen,
lies the realm where life convenes.
With spirits open, hearts aligned,
we step into a boundless bind.

Each stride forward, a journey begun,
into the domains yet to be spun.
Exploring depths of mind and soul,
we seek to comprehend the whole.

So let us journey, fearless and true,
embracing the mystery of the new.
For in the expanse of what lies beyond,
we discover the magic of life's endless bond.

Closing Reflections

To all the cherished readers of Soulful Musings, I extend my heartfelt gratitude. It is my sincere wish that these poems have reached the depths of your soul, offering solace, inspiration, and a profound connection to the human experience we all share.

As I conclude this journey, my heart overflows with gratitude. Together, through poetry, we've explored emotions, embraced introspection, and reveled in the beauty of language. Thank you for embracing my words and allowing them to resonate within you.

May the echoes of these poems linger in your heart, serving as a perpetual reminder of the enduring allure and transformative power of written expression. THANK YOU for accompanying me on this soulful voyage.

In ink-stained reverence,

Aishwarya Damodar